MALALA

poems by

LYN LIFSHIN

POETIC MATRIX PRESS

Front Cover photo of Malala Yousafzai

By Jussi K. Niemela

jussikniemela.blogspot.com

Poetic Matrix Press
www.poeticmatrix.com

MALALA

The story of Malala and her struggles is gripping; this account is a work of poetry by Lyn Lifshin, an important American poet. This is not journalism, rather it is a work that is best suited for poetry, a deeply personal work where the poet reveals, through compassion and insight, some moments of revelation. The people it discusses are real, but the insights and details are poetic. The events in this book are contemporary and sometimes controversial and it is the poets mandate to present the depth of her understanding and then allow the work to speak for itself.

The Publisher

CONTENTS

DARK BIRDS OF HER DREAMS:
(WARNINGS, UNEASE)

SUDDENLY THE WALLS SEEM FRAGILE,
DRIFTING AWAY: (GROWING TERROR)

WHAT SOME HAVE SAID ABOUT THIS BOOK

Once more Lyn Lifshin, the American queen of the small press scene for the last forty years, makes her voice heard, this time in support of Malala Yousafzai, an innocent Pakistani school girl who in 2008 at a press conference in Peshawar asked why the Taliban was taking away her right to basic education.

What religion or ideology can justify the attempt to murder a 15 year old girl who speaks out for education? This new book by Lyn Lifshin is both brave and innovative. The poet somehow teleports herself to Pakistan and reaches across the oceans to enter the mind of 15 year old Malaya. The reader sees the moment as Malaya does. The poems are a breath of fresh air in a world that is filled with poison. Malaya's voice is the voice of hope and innocence.

— Toni Ortner has 13 books and has been published in over 100 literary magazines.

These are some of the most powerful and passionate poems ever to be taken to paper. Lifshin unearths mounds of history and builds it back up aside the heroic actions of one young woman. A woman who should be the subject of poem after poem, day after day!

Lifshin may have created her most astounding work yet. She opened a door into history and when you peek in, it falls all over.

Lifshin's look inside Pakistan is unique, as it brings beauty to a hard history; it brings comfort to cruelty.

— Candace Chouinard poet, editor

With the fervor and passion that only a true poet can wield, Lyn Lifshin writes about Malala Yousafzai's near-tragedy as the "Dark birds of her dreams plung-ing/in flame onto hillsides/that once looked as if they'd been dipped in beauty" in a paean to hope, innocence, and the rights of all females everywhere. In this book Lifshin becomes the essence of Malala, the great longing for a future that each person builds with their own characterizing spirit. She, along side Malala, cries out for the justice that should allow all of us to individualize and love life so much that "each day could unravel new mysteries."

— Christina Zawadiwsky is Ukrainian-American, born in New York City, is a poet, artist, journalist, critic and TV producer.

CROSS ROADS AND LIMBO:

(The Long Winter Waiting to Heal)

AS ROOTS OF NEW FLOWERS CAN'T HELP
BUT PUSH UP PAST DEAD LEAVES,
MALALA IS BLOOMING AGAIN:
(Recovery and new Beginnings)

AUTHOR BIOGRAPHY

PRESS PRODUCERS

MALALA

When Malala Yousafzai slipped her pink dress over her dark curls that October 9th morning in 2012, neither she, nor anyone who knew her, could have imagined how radically changed and different her life would be from that afternoon on. It would be a long time, if ever, before she could slip back into her room and the bed she had called her own in the Swat District of Pakistan's northwestern Khyber Pakhtunkhwa province.

It's not that she wasn't aware of the Taliban's cruelty and tortures, how they had banned girls from going to school. As early as September 2008 her father took her to Peshawar to speak at the local press club. "How dare the Taliban take away my basic right to education?" she told the audience. Her speech was covered by newspapers and television throughout the area. In early 2009 Malala wrote a blog under a pseudonym for the BBC about life under Taliban rule and their attempts to take control of the valley. Wild for education as Malala was, outspoken and strong as her need to continue to learn, nothing could stop her passion for this freedom to continue. Editors at BBC agreed, since another girl had agreed to write a diary but then felt it was too dangerous, that Malala, four years younger than the original volunteer, and in 7th grade at the time, would take her place. BBC had been covering the violence and politics in Swat in detail and didn't know much about how ordinary people lived under the Taliban. Because they were concerned about Yousafzai's safety, they insisted she use a pseudonym. She was published under the byline "Gul Makai, cornflower in Urdu, a name taken from a character in a Pashtun folk tale.

In 2009 the first part of a New York Times documentary, *Class Dismissed,* was filmed about her life in Pakistan. Malala began to give interviews in print and on TV. In many ways the documentary ironically predicts not only the challenges Malala will meet for her brave efforts to defend the basic rights of children in Pakistan, namely the right of girls to education, making her very vulnerable, tragically, but also her determination and strength to fight to fulfill her dreams.

She took a position as chair person of the District Child Assembly Swat and was nominated for the International Children's Peace Prize in 2011 by Desmond Tuto and in 2013 Malala was nominated for The Nobel Peace Prize. Malala did not win the International Children's Peace Prize for 2011, but was awarded the National Peace Award by the Pakistan government that same year. In April 29, 2013 she was featured on the cover of Time as one of the short list for Most Important People of the year. In 2013 she spoke at the United Nations, met President Obama and Queen Elizabeth. She won the Mother Teresa Memorial Award for Social Justine, Rome Prize for Peace and Action, Simone de Beauvoir Prize, Honorary Canadian Citizen as well as many other awards from around the world and dedications from a variety of famous celebrities.

But that afternoon, politics must have been the last thing on her mind, as giggling with friends and singing on the bus home from school that October 9, 2012 the bus jolted to a stop. *Which one of you is Malala* one gunman screamed.

In her documentary Malala asked why innocents are targets, why peace is burning in this village, once a beautiful resort where people made reservations way in advance to dine in gorgeous hotels in breathtakingly beautiful surroundings and shop in the most prized, luxurious shops. Suddenly, in this ghost town many left out of terror, Malala was shot in the head and neck by a Taliban gunman.

She remained unconscious and in critical condition for days, but alive. On October 12, a group of 50 Islamic clerics issued a fatwa against those who tried to kill her but most Pakistani government officials have refrained from publicly criticizing the Taliban by name over the attack in what critics say is a lack of resolve against extremism. The Taliban justified their attack as part of religious scripture, saying that the "Quran says that people propagating {sic} against Islam and Islamic forces would be killed," going on to say "Sharia says that even a child can be killed if she is propagating [sic]against Islam." [1]

The experience of Malala is only one aspect of Pakistan and its culture and now its history. From reports I have read, most of the Taliban activity is in the administrative district of Swat, which is a relatively small part of Pakistan. This series of poems is not intended to describe all of Pakistan with its rich history and varied culture or to discuss politics. I understand that there are strong and divergent opinions about the causes of the Taliban actions.

Whatever Malala chooses to do, it promises to be extraordinary: whether she pursues her original hope of being a doctor or continues to be a role model and an advocate for education and for girls' and women's rights.

[1] The Express Tribune with the International New York Times
"Taliban says its attack on Malala justified" by Reuters Published October 16, 2012

RUSHING TO THE METRO ALREADY A LITTLE LATE ON MY WAY TO BALLET I NEARLY SKID ON ACORNS, CATCH MYSELF

I think of Malala, maybe rushing, never
wanting to think her name means "grief
stricken," as I've written a poem about
becoming what you're called. Maybe
she was humming a song she heard once
on TV before the Taliban made it a crime.
Or she was watching leaves drift from the bus
or giggling with girl friends. Maybe
she was thinking of being a doctor and
coming back to treat young children
in her region, her swat. Or maybe she
was hoping to see a certain boy with
licorice eyes and a smile who always
made her giggle. No longer able to wear
school uniforms, told to wear plain
clothes, Malala wrote in her blog,
"Instead, I decided to wear my favorite
pink dress." Maybe the last beautiful
thing she saw as the bullet entered her
mahogany curls, until later she woke
up in the hospital's cone of light.

DARK BIRDS OF HER DREAMS:
(WARNINGS, UNEASE)

ONCE A HAVEN FOR HONEYMOONERS, THE SWITZERLAND OF PAKISTAN

Malala must have
loved the beauty
of the mountains,
afternoons near
the lake, ancient
trees, lying down
among flowers face
to face with emerald
leaves. She had
entered a new world
of books, of young
women in other
countries in
exotic clothes
with the same
feelings that
leaped in her blood.
She knew books were
a friend, never
a threat but a
warm comforting
rose scented bath
she could enter and
soak in, come out,
relaxed, and new.

IN HER DREAM

the blue black mountains
explode with date palms
and ephedra. There are
freeze frames before the
killer when she floated
among water hyacinths.
Red fox and wild boar
skittered thru tamarisk
and reeds, camels, deer,
gazelles slithered thru
those wet lands with
pelicans and gull and
no one, nothing to make
her feel that no one was
supposed to hear what
she was singing.

LIKE CHILDREN TRAILING GLORY

Malala, still playing with dolls,
believed she could change the
world, cure cancer, live on the
moon, make a difference in
the world. Did she imagine that
some day those who
believe in violence could
share the same sky's
beauty, that the light of
childhood could bring
a glow to darkness?

MALALA'S THIRD DREAM OF MILITARY HELICOPTERS

no longer throwing
toffee from the sky
but filling the air
with darkness. She
could hear artillery
fire. By morning
only half the girls kept
coming to school.
On her way home
she heard a man say
"I will kill you." It
sounded like a
requiem. Withered
leaves fell thru
her hair as if she
was still dreaming.
Dark birds of her
dreams plunging
in flame on to hill-
sides that once
looked as if they'd
been dipped in beauty.

WHEN SHE HEARD THEY WANTED

to close the schools, Sept 2008,
she spoke to a local press club,
asked how the Taliban can take
away her basic right to an
education. And when an older
girl's family wouldn't let her
write a blog, Malala wrote "our
annual exams are due after vacation
but this will only be possible if the
Taliban allow girls to go to school."
That's when she began having bad
dreams about headless bodies of
police hung in the town square.

SHE SAID SHE COULDN'T SEE TO WALK EASILY

in her long gray
drab burqua. Some
times it was hot.
It was as if she
wanted to bring
color, not the
source of the storm,
wanted to walk
into life like it
was her house. She
wanted to wear
pink because
it was her favorite
color. There are
songs she wants
to sing. She wants
to feel as if each
day could unravel
new mysteries.
She wants the school
to receive her in
quiet calmness the
way the lake
opens to receive
a flock of swans.

WHEN THEY BANNED MUSIC

it was as if even
birds' songs were
about to be crushed.
On the road to
Bann, when the bus
hit a pothole her
ten year old
brother thought
it was a bomb blast.
When the family
traveled from
Islamabad to
Lahore, her 5
year old brother, when
asked what he was
doing, said he
was digging a grave.

THE FULL MOON PULLS OUT

dreams like silk
pajamas. Dark
silk dreams of
her fathers death
thread the wind.
When her father
forgets her birthday,
she ridicules
him in a text
message, forces
him to apologize
and to buy everyone
a round of
ice cream.

THE TALIBAN — WHO DO NOT REPRESENT TRUE ISLAM — SAY IT WAS FOR PROTECTION AND SECURITY

they say punishment
is permitted in
Islam all the while
young boys are bleeding
and screaming. They
say the boards shake under
each lash as the dozen
Taliban start holding
Kalashnikovs and
rocket launchers.

EVEN WHEN NOT SHOT BY THE TALIBAN, WITH THEIR BACKWARD, BRUTAL "LAWS"

girls going to school
are in danger. Hours
of inconceivable terror.
Many are raped, sexually
assaulted or abducted.
Some, before they've
learned to love things
as they never were sure
or supposed they might
be victimized by
teachers, school staff
or classmates. Parents
pull their daughters
as wild flowers open,
not wanting to risk
further violence. The
girls have a hard time
learning when they
fear guns. Deep
gender bias is reflected
in classrooms, in
teaching methods, the
curriculum. Schools
do not have separate
bathrooms, leading them
to drop out. When
money is tight at home,

boys come first. Girls
view education as
a frill. They stay at
home to care for siblings,
cook, work the farm.
After finishing hours of
chores after school,
study into the
night with little or
no electricity,
only the stars.

AFTER EXPLORING THE WRECKAGE

classrooms that
the military had
turned into a
bunker after they
pushed the
Taliban out of the
Swat Valley.
Creeping closer to
the window
Malala noticed
how soldiers
drilled a lookout
hole into the wall
of her classroom,
scribbling on the
wall with yellow
high lighter
"look this is
Pakistan, Taliban
destroyed us."
The words
glisten like a
wild animal's fur.
In her latest
email, all in

caps, she wrote, I
WANT ACCESS
TO THE WORLD
OF KNOWLEDGE
and she signed it
your small video star.

STILL IN HER AUGUST INTERVIEW

Malala showed hope
for her country, a
hope Pakistan wanted
to preserve. "When I
see the current
situation here," she
says, "I thank God for
the peace that prevails
and that girls can
attend school," not
able to imagine evil
with a thick black
pelt slithering thru
branches like
a madman.

WHEN SHE HEARD THE MAN

threaten to kill her.
When her pink dress
felt like a shroud
and then she turned
around and saw
he was talking to
someone else on
his cell phone,
realized he must
have been
threatening someone
different over
the phone. Terror
melted from her skin
as if she'd been
dipping in rose
scented
calming warm
water.

A YEAR AFTER THE FILMMAKER

did a two part documentary
on her family, Malala and
her father stayed with the
filmmaker in Islamabad
where she once went
shopping for English
language books and dvd's,
picked up some trashy
American sitcom books.
The filmmaker had to remind
herself that this girl, who
never shuddered at
beheaded corpses,
public flogging
or death threats at her
father, was still just a kid.

ONCE THE CHILDREN PLAYED

games with wooden
cylinders — blue, red
and yellow. You
can't get out of prison
until a 6 is rolled. All
sorts of intricate
rules. The children
played under
date palms and
tamarisk and in
the wet lands of
the Indus River
Delta. Now they
play being
suicide bombers.

SUDDENLY THE WALLS SEEM FRAGILE, DRIFTING AWAY: (GROWING TERROR)

SO FEARLESS, CHANTING WITH OTHER SCHOOL GIRLS

in the school yard
the last day before
school's done
along the sun
drenched roads.
Again and again.
until next time
God willing. Then
helicopters and
guns turn the air to
dust, birds
explode up from
the flowers. Many
crash dead. Blood
and petals. A war
zone of flowers.
This hide and
seek goes on all
night. We are very
afraid. This, Malala
writes, is my life.

BEFORE THE TALIBAN CLOSED DOWN HER SCHOOL IN THE SWAT VALLEY

the war displaced her
family, her friends.
Nights in a house
with no books, only
the stars for company.
Lying alone in the
dark not able to sleep,
she must have listened
to night birds. If
there were dreams,
they were dreams of
those girls screaming,
acid thrown in their face.
Then waking up in
a house she no longer
knew where everything
stood, terrified about
her school, her two
pet chickens.

THE TALIBAN TRIED TO KILL HER

You could see darkness growing as the
leaves were changing, how they left
scorched bark, blood spattered on cedar.
They threw acid on the
faces of other
girls seeking to learn.
Even the trees would
have run. Vultures,
falcons, pheasants,
swirl of blood rose in
the force of the storm
leaving, the body of
a 7 year old wrapped
in stained cloth.

AS IF HOPE WAS A GIFT OF STRUGGLE

Suddenly, from all
the lushness
around her,
something she
doesn't quite
know what to call
it has disappeared. She
feels it in browning
flowers, in the lost
chickens and
feathers. After 3
months of separation
the family is reunited
in the Swat Valley
and Malala pleads
with the US Ambassador
to help, please, in our
education. Suddenly
the walls seem
fragile, drifting away.
But she holds on to
Benazir Bhutte as her
inspiration.

IN THE NEW SHARIA LAW

women were
not allowed to
go to jobs or
markets.

Malala was sent
to the country to
live with
relatives.

"I am really
bored," she wrote,
"because I have no
books."

NIGHTS BEFORE SHARIA LAW BECOMES MORE STRICT

Malala wrote in
her blog, quoting
her younger brother,
"oh God bring
peace to Swat and
if not, then bring
either the US or
China here."

FEB 21, 2009

Malala got what
she'd been hoping
for so long: Fazula
announced on his
FM station that he
was lifting the ban on
women's education
and girls would be
allowed to attend
school until exams
were heard. But
they had to wear
burqas.

IN FEBRUARY MALALA

wrote on her blog
that she and her
class played a lot
and enjoyed life as
usual. Helicopters
didn't appear as
often, their dark
shadows on the
jade lace trees.
There were no
whispers of the
Taliban. The size
of the class was up.
But in two days the
Taliban were
breaking down
the peace deal,
mortar shells rang
thru the night.
Malala's brother
was afraid to go to
school, afraid of
being kidnapped.

"MY DREAM BOY WILL COME TO MARRY ME"
—— Malala sprawled in front of her TV before the Taliban
  restricted as much as they could

a break from
gunshots in the streets
of Mingora. Her father
said, "don't be scared,
this is firing the
peace." He had read in
the newspapers that
the Taliban announced
they were going to
sign a peace deal the
next day. Then another
round of firing
started outside.
People believe
more in what
the militants
say, not the
government
When they
heard the news
Malala's mother
and father started
to cry and her
two younger
brothers had
tears in their eyes.

WHEN MALALA RETURNED HOME, FEBRUARY 2009

there was an
eerie silence.
The streets
were deserted.
When they
went to the
supermarket
to get a gift
for her mother
it was closed.
Other shops
were closed.
Their house had
been burglarized,
their TV stolen.

GUL MAKAI

a Pashto word for corn
flower, the name of
a heroine in local
Pakistani folk tales.
No wonder Malala
chose that secret pen
name in Urdu, a
name closer to her
dreams. Once life
became hell, as she
wrote in January 2009,
My Swat is beautiful,
but there is no peace.
Like an underground
online railroad, she would
pass what she wrote to a
reporter. Scanned and
emailed, they were printed
on the BBC, startling
as an s.o.s. tossed from
a speeding car of a kid-
napper in still fresh blood.
Special, her father
said from the start, his
July born precious ruby.
Gentle, rare, beautiful.
She should have been free
to watch the patterns of

stars and mountains high
over Islamabad, dream
of being a pilot or
maybe a doctor.

SUDDENLY EVERYTHING LOVELY
HAS DISAPPEARED: (Malala's Shot)

LIKE ANY BULLY STAKING A CLAIM, TREATENING, HIDEOUS

in the chill, uncertain dawn,
the Talilan, driven out of
Swat, want to prove
they have a presence.
Like any bully, they're wild
to show they can still
maim, carry out attacks,
terrify the area. Like wild
beasts, menacing and
sullenly they need to prove
they have not been wiped
out, can target what they
consider symbolic targets,
prove the government is
not in control, will pick a
young girl coming out of a
school bus maybe in a
pink dress, color
of a flower.

ON THAT DAY

the teenagers
chattered with their
teachers as the school
bus rattled along the
country road. They
just finished a term
paper and broke out
singing a Pashton
song. That music must
have been the last
thing Malala heard,
one of the last she
remembers.
Two men flagged down
the bus, boarded,
screamed. *Which one
is Malala?* Silence.
The rust leaves all
that moved in the
breeze. The girls,
terrified, frozen. Only
their eyes moved to
Malala.
That one the gun
man said. Fired two
shots. Then he fled.
The Teacher said

Drive
to the local hospital,
stared in horror at
Malala's body, bleeding
and bleeding, unconscious
in her friend's lap.

I THINK OF THE YOUNG GIRL

Malala collapsed on
after the second
shot,

her lap soaked with
her friend's blood.

What she'll remember
longer than the sight

of minarets and
lanterns against

a pink and
green blue
black sky,

longer than singing:
The red stain

spreading, the
warm wetness,

the smell of Malala's hair.

ON OCTOBER 9, 2012

a Taliban gunman shot Malala Yousafzai
as she rode home on a bus
after taking an exam in
Pakistan's Swat Valley. *"Which*
of you is Malala? Speak up,
otherwise I'll shoot you all."
When he found out which
girl was Malala he shot her twice.
Once in the head and once
in the neck.

FOR MONTHS A TEAM OF TALIBAN SHARPSHOOTERS

studied the daily route
Malala took to school.
Camouflaged by
orchid trees and
jasmine, by purple
flowering trees in
sunset light, they
tracked her smile, bright
clothes and giggling.
Then when she was
bleeding and slumped,
the Tehrik-e Taliban
gleefully claimed
responsibility saying
Malala was an
American spy who
idolized the "black
devil Obama"
and her blood hadn't
yet dried on the school
bus floor when they
vowed to shoot her
again should she
survive.

AFTER THE ATTACK

as if she'd been wild to
make love to all
learning in ways that
hadn't been, as if she
was something flying
gorgeous and free,
white feathers in the
light in widening circles,
suddenly she is a crumpled
feathers, a shot down
swan.
In some photos,
from a hospital in
Mingora,
the young girl seems a
lump, surrounded by police
and cameras, wrapped in
a bloody sheet.
Hours ago she was
giggling, singing.
The military
press later released photos
of soldiers evacuating
Malala and tending to
her in another
hospital. You could
not tell if she was
even alive.

AS THE LIGHT BEGAN TO GO AWAY

when the bullet entered
what was the last thing
Malala saw fading to
darkness? The slash
of the gunman's
eyes? A sneer,
smoke? Or was it the
blue peaks? Capped
with snow, Juniper
and Chir Pine?
The Bahrain hills?
Pakola storm
trees? Or the
pigeons, flushed
up out of the
dusky roses
and thistles?

SUDDENLY EVERYTHING LOVELY HAS DISAPPEARED

After the shooting she
was air lifted to a
military hospital in
Peshawar where doctors
were forced to begin
operating after swelling
developed in the left
portion of her brain,
damaged when the
bullet passed thru her
head. After a 3 hour
surgery they successfully
removed the bullet
that lodged in her
shoulder near her
spinal cord. Suddenly
all who loved her
were so afraid.

ONLY YEARS FROM WHEN SHE HELD A DOLL

in the curve of
her body. She flares
up like a flame,
makes her own
shadow she can
move in, lets everything
happen to her
like an exploding
tree, beauty and
horror, the terror of
the Taliban's "even
a child should be
killed" and then the
faces making a
bracelet around her,
the first light
opening her eyes.

EVEN AFTER THE SHOOTING MOST PAKISTAN OFFICERS DID NOT CRITICIZE THE TALIBAN

She was still treated
in the intensive care
unit. She was
moving her arms
and legs, responded
to her teacher right
after the shooting.
On October 11 a panel
of Pakistani and
British doctors made
the decision to move
her to the Armed
Forces Institute of
Cardiology. A
medical team
treating her at
the hospital said
she has a 70 percent
chance of recovery.
According to her
uncle she has not been
responsive or
conscious
since the surgery
to remove the
bullet and
remained on
the ventilator.

PHYSICAL SCARS, EMOTIONAL SCARS

On October 9 Kainat
Rins left her high school
and climbed into the
back of a small van.
Driving thru lacy green
lantana, the girls
chattering in the sun
suddenly felt the van jolt
and stop. A masked gun
emerged like a shadow.
The girls started
screaming. "Be still," the
man hissed. "*Where is
Malala?*" It happened so
fast. Blood was coming
from her ear. The gun
man kept firing, Kainat
was shot. 13 year old
Shazia too. Everyone
crying, trying to lift
Malala. Bullets in the
slim girl's hand. No one
would sleep for nights.
Even the town, once lush
and green, now was
wounded.

AS THE DAYS MOVE FROM DARKNESS TO LIGHT: (MALALA'S MONTHS IN HOSPITAL)

WHEN SHE FIRST CAME TO

did the white of hospital
walls blind her? Did she
touch her neck, touch
gauze instead of skin?
Were there snow capped
hills, sky blue as the
tawny blue sky in
Lahore? The hum of
sparrows nothing like
wind blowing thru
skinny jade pines and purple
roses still unstained with
gun powder, blood
and only the sun moving
like a tongue thru
shadows?

ON THE DAY THE FIRST PICTURES OF MALALA
IN THE BRITISH HOSPITAL WERE SHOWN

People held babies and
signs that said "I am
Malala."
Grandmothers,
children, mothers, a
girl of 14. Some with
head scarves, some
bare headed . One
light glowed like a
sun, a
yellow jewel or
beacon. "Malala said
what so many of us
wish to
say but are afraid,
so many
kidnapped, raped
and shot."

WEEKS LYING IN THE HOSPITAL COVE

warm and clean.
Still she misses
her pet chicken,
the jagged mountain
peaks topped
with snow, the
Swat river.
Someone reads, her
attacker hates
everything western:
the music, the
books, any
women who can read.
He believes that
polio and the vaccine
are part of a conspiracy
of the Jews
and Christians
to make Moslems
impotent. She
hears he rides thru
towns pointing
weapons
in the air and ordering
motorists to remove
the tape decks in
their car. Fazulullah,
like his Taliban
predecessors, deem

music and anything that
plays music un-Islamic.
Malala wonders
about this man.
If he had a daughter
could he shoot
her in the neck
and head? Throw
acid in her face
and eyes.

CARDS SPILL FROM HER HOSPITAL BED

get well cards,
we love you.
Malala stares
ahead. Who
knows what
she's thinking
trapped but
safer in her
hospital room,
imagining,
maybe she is
butterfly free,
beautiful as
the lemon
butterfly or the
red spit Jazel.
Maybe
she is going thru
the names of
butterflies her
father talked
about, cabbage
white
butterfly, plain
tiger, grass yellow
wings in the sun
light of those
days when
she still glowed
like a lamp —
so much
brightness coming
from inside.

MOVING TOWARD THE SOLSTICE

as the holiday wraps
Birmingham hospital
in bright lights and
music. Early
December, 2012.

"What country am I in?"
This strange land of
snow with more music
than she ever imagined,

more cards than
she can read, more
food, more pastries,
more bright clothes,
more

dolls and teddy bears
than she could ever
hug.

I THINK OF MALALA IN HER HOSPITAL ROOM

as leaves flutter
and wither.
Before snow
camouflages
wounds, I wonder
if she can yet see
the most
beautiful things
coming out from
underneath things
she didn't know
she could get out
from underneath,
her eyes opening
even wider like the
earliest buds on
the camellia branches.

AS DAYS GET DARKER

moving toward the shortest
day of the year Malala's
brothers must feel rootless
out of school. So many
strange accents. So damp
and gray. Lonely without
friends romping in acacia
and jasmine. So many
days waiting in hospital
corridors or stark rooms.
Edgy, scared. Afraid for
their sister. Then the
oddness of strangers'
eyes, the weirdness
of TV and reporters.
The food that doesn't
taste like their food.
The music, so different.
No one speaks Pastung.
The games are so
different. But all that
matters is their sister,
the flicker of a
smile, her eyes.

AS THE DAYS GET BLACK

earlier, Malala's
brothers thought of
going back to school.
There wouldn't be
guns and helicopters
to be afraid of. But
how can they not be
scared, a new
language, children
who may smile but
speak in different terms.
It was one thing
for their sister to
say "I am afraid of
no one." And all
the people sending
her gifts. But to
move into a school
where all the
children know each
other, know
English, history
and customs and
they are like two little
boys who have already
been treated and
wounded in
ways you can't see.
It's scary.

MONTHS NOW IN THE HOSPITAL ROOM

Malala watches snow
against the pewter
sky,

Maybe she sighs,
the days blurring,
thinking how long until
it will truly be as the

the Koran says,
and the "fringe minority

of darkness," of hatred,
of conflict where

extremists fear a girl
with a book in her hand

will be no more.

THAT SPARK

there in her
eyes. You can
see it in the
films, on the
verge of, just
waiting to
explode, be
there, a flame
unfolding,
catching every -
thing
in its path, a
gorgeous
bloom, it's
contagious,
it puts its
arm around you.
If this isn't a
kiss that will
shut out the
world, bring in
the world, make
a bracelet of
the world then
what is the word
for it. Some-
thing about Malala,
everyone
saw it.
Nothing can
make
it go away.

THAT CERTAIN SPARK

like some jewel in the
sand, blue diamond tossed
on snow or, say, stained
glass twisting grey light
strawberry and lime on my
mother's lamps. Something
about how it lit up the
room. Something about her
eyes, her smile transformed
the way I'd lie out barrettes
made of old crystal and
Czech beads on the bed at
4 o'clock and watch how
the sun turned
the rubies to fire. Some
voices do it. I've saved
answering machine tapes—
its that spark, mysterious—
Malala's father saw it in
her and won't believe it
can ever go.

WE ARE WAITING, HOPING FOR THE SPARK TO COME BACK

only 11 when she began
blogging entries from
her diary. Gul Makai,
the name she took,
corn flower in Pashto.
One of the best students
with licorice bushy
eyebrows and intense
mahogany eyes. She
wrote about the headless
bodies hanging in the
square, how she
hid school books under
her shawl and how
she kept reading even
after the Taliban
outlawed school for
girls. In January 2009
her teacher told the
girls not to wear
colorful dresses that
might make them even
more angry. Tho
her father has two
other younger boys, he
says there is something
about Malala so
unique, a certain spark.

IN THE DOCUMENTARY

There is a wildness,
that electricity in her
eyes, that impish
grin. In the
documentary you
expect any minute
her face will crinkle
into an explosive smile.
Even when she is
afraid for her father,
even when he spends
the night somewhere
it might be safe or
she says smiling, "I'd
hide in the bathroom,
in the cupboard." Her
eyes black fire,
sparkling, so alive
and bright
as jewels. Still a beauty
in her hospital quilts
and stuffed animals
but I want her back in
those burgundy colors,
in the fearless, funny
way — darting all over
like a hummingbird
that can't get enough
of what its after.

FAIRY MEADOWS AT NANGO PARBAT

She remembers how
they look like
Paradise, clear blue
sky. An enormous
bulk of
ice and rock. Lush
green pines, alpine
pastures in
summer.
Malala thinks of
the stillness there,
walking through silver
fir and blue pine
without fear of
men with guns.
Paradise to walk
to school,
enchantment to
feel the sun
through thick
wool.

ON MALALA DAY

Her young schoolmates
prayed and lit candles.
Her face, large
mahogany eyes pleading,
searching, still remind
me of that student in the
slow class, the ones with
boys on parole and
girls who couldn't stop
giggling and
chattering
and Ramona, as lilting
a name as Malala's and
as dazed as the wounded
girl looks in some
photos, puzzled
how
things came to this,
when, like Malala, in the
middle of class boys
and girls jump on
desks, stream into the
hall, she with her 70 IQ,
sat primly, attentively
at her desk moaning
"I want
to learn," as if that
should not be
impossible.

STILL CLUTCHING A TEDDY BEAR

her eyes enormous. Most of the
time she doesn't smile,
a deer caught in
headlights.
I can't imagine her
mother's heart isn't
racing, seeing her
once again
in nightmares,
walking to the bus. I
can't imagine her
hearing the Taliban
threats over and over
in Swat never
being able
to sleep again.

I LOVE HER AND LAST NIGHT WHEN WE MET THERE WERE TEARS IN OUR EYES, OUT OF HAPPINESS

Malala's
father says it was a miracle
that she lives, that she survived.
First he says,
I thought I
was preparing for a funeral.
Then I laughed at it because
of all our sacrifices. My
personal sacrifices. This attack
on my daughter can
not be such a cheap
purpose we would go to
some other country to live the rest
of our lives there.

I THINK OF HER FATHER

vowing to bring Malala
home. When he sees scars on
her neck, the jagged line
where
a necklace could sparkle,
doesn't the threats scare
him?
I think of her in the hospital
still clutching stuffed
animals, how she wanted to
be a doctor
but he convinced
her politics mattered more.
Too young in this
country to get her ears
pierced or drive, too young
to date, still he dreams of
bringing her back to where
she's unprotected as a
deer in hunting season,
iridescent in
screaming coral and
violet.

WHEN SHE HEARS

of the young Afghan
woman beheaded for
refusing
to become a prostitute,
Malala shivers in her clean
hospital room at the news.
Before she stops shivering,
another story as horrid of
a young woman who, when
she wouldn't become a
whore, was knifed to
death by her 18 year
old cousin days after
another girl was
tortured and killed, her
nose, ears
and fingers cut off
before she was murdered.

HER FATHER MUST BE STUNNED
AT THE FORCE OF THIS STORM

he still wants his
daughter out in the
world, a leader, risking
danger. But what of her
mother? Does she wish
she could pull her back
into the cove of her
body and not feel this
fear and loneliness begin?

BECAUSE SHE PROMOTED WESTERN THINKING

because she wanted
to learn, the Taliban
vows to finish the
job in the future.
Because, as horrid,
the American congress
woman, Gifford, who
was shot by another
man who couldn't
bear to have people
in love with life live,
did everything he
could to change that.
Because who can
believe anyone who
didn't hate themselves
could do so much
harm to anyone else

IN PAKISTAN AMID SECURITY FEAR

in one photograph
a flicker of a
smile on the
wounded girl's
face. But in
Mingora, shadow
of future Taliban
reprisals dark as a
terrible black
tree of knives and
blood means the
school girls can
not answer her
in public.
Children lit
candles, held
special prayers.
The Taliban say
they will attack
any girl who
stands against
them. Speaking to
the media could put
lives in danger but
Asma Khan, 12,
said, *after the*
attack, we now
have more courage

73

to study
and now we will
fulfill her
mission to spread
education
for everyone.

MALALA EXPECTED TO MAKE BRITAIN
HER PERMANENT HOME

because of his
experience as
a teacher and
an administrative
role in Pakistan, the
Pakistani government
has now
offered Malala's
father
a new position
with a home in
Birmingham, and a
car. People feel
they have a
duty to care for
her, feel the
situation in
Pakistan is
too dangerous.

WHEN SHE IS WELL

they tell her she can stroll in Sutton
Park, fearlessly, in her pink dress,
not the burka-like clothes it's hard
to see in, easy to trip. She listens to
stories about famous painters and their
seascapes, how music she's never heard
was popular here in the 1960s. When
she hears there are famous art collectors,
she asks for books with the history of art
and music. Such luxuries she could curl
to sleep with!
And tho she is fascinated hearing there
is a planetarium and a collection that
includes the Smethwick Engine, the
world's oldest working steam engine, I can
imagine her smiling, knowing Cadbury
World shows visitors stages and steps
and I bet she is sure there
are samples.

CROSS ROADS AND LIMBO:
(THE LONG WINTER WAITING TO HEAL)

AFTER THE GLITTER OF CHRISTMAS LIGHTS AND TINSEL

does Malala drift into
dreams of being who
she was, dazed as if
she'd been circling
for years, doesn't know
where she is. The book
on the bed, unopened,
bandages on her skin
you don't see.

IF EVEN A CHURCH OFERING TO PRAY

for the teenage
activist is a target for
violence demanding
$51,000
or else they will
destroy
the building and
every one inside it

AFTER "A DAMAGED SKULL AND INTENSIVE NEURO-REHABILITATION" SPRING FLOWERS OPEN IN A VASE NEAR HER BED

I think of her waking
from a nightmare
screaming out in
a language none of
the nurses know.
Sometimes her
sadness is dark as
ravens or crows until
suddenly she sees the
sky and sees the
beauty of falling stars
and moves deep into
the quilts
and hopes to sleep.

MILES FROM THE COUNTRY SHE CALLED NORMAL LIFE

does Malala listen
to news? Pakistan
pulls on her, no
feelings are final.
Can she imagine
the Taliban snarl
how media
showed bias. How
they screamed
this filthy godless
media has
taken huge advantage
of the situation,
journalists have
started passing
judgment. Does
she still dream
she can reach out
across
the world?

SHE INSISTS ON HAVING A BOOK

in her lap, the
shawl
covering what
bullets
twisted. This
crossroad,
this limbo.
Can she, as
Rilke says, go
to the
limits of longing,
let everything
happen, beauty
and terror
and keep on.

IF SOME DAYS ARE BITTER

what she has already
done must turn bleak
days to wine. What is
it like, the intensity of
loss and strangeness,
wondering, not sure
what is ahead. If she
can ever go back to
Pakistan, go back
to herself.

EARLIER IN NOVEMBER PARLIAMENT
INTRODUCED LEGISLATION

for compulsory
education for both boys
and girls, making it a
crime to
keep a child at home,
offending parents can be
fined up to 500$. Still,
earlier this month the
Taliban attacked a bus
load of girls returning
from school in the tribal
regions, throwing acid
in their faces, they
were accused of
embracing the west
through education.

I DON'T THINK SHE WILL COME TO EDUCATION ANY MORE IN SWAT

she will not be safe
here. Now she is a
celebrity said one
friend. There is for
Malala's attacker
no justice, no arrest.
Nothing has
happened to him.
The outrage her
shooting started has
subsided without
any real changes.

SHE IS GETTING BETTER EVERYDAY

and asks about all of us and
what we are doing says 15 year
old Mahnon, one of Malala's
closest friends. *When it*
happened we just cried and
prayed. We weren't worried
about ourselves. We were just
worried for her. 12 year old
Emar said of the
Taliban, *They are thinking*
she is a girl and can't do
anything. In a strong
voice and speaking English, Gulrana, a
17 year old,
said students have gotten
courageous. Malala
and everyone is attending
school. No one stays home. She
said the attack has turned the
country
against extremists
and now every girl is saying, *I*
want to be Malala.
Her father says the family
will return to Pakistan. But
even her classmates worry for
her safety.

BOTH THE ARMY AND POLICE

are deployed outside
the school whose
name means
"happy." Journalists
were not permitted
to pass
its black iron gate
until last week
when reporters and
photographers were
let inside.
Authorities feared
drawing attention
but the students seemed un-
concerned. After
offering words of
support and saying they
weren't afraid to
come to the school,
even the shyest
girls would whisper
to a friend "tell
her not to stop
studying.

AT MALALA'S OLD SCHOOL

the students are quick to attack
the Taliban and display a giant
poster of Malala. The
school, which has more than
500 students, only closed
its doors briefly at the
height of the Taliban's hold
on the region in 2008 and
early 2009. It was then that
Malala began to blog,
recording her unhappiness with
Taliban edicts aimed at girls
in her school. Only 9 at the time,
Shazia remembers those
days. Times were very bad.
Girls hiding their books under
burqas. Compared to then, now
is a very good time she
says, her pink shawl covering
her head. "We are strong."

ONE GIRL WHO WANTS TO BECOME A DOCTOR

is a stubborn teenager.
She doesn't want police
escorts. "They say 1
need the police. But 1
say 1 don't need any,"
she says pushing her
glasses firmly back on
her nose. "1 didn't want
police to come with me
to school because 1
will stand out from other
students. But 1
shouldn't."

QUICK TO LAUGH

Kainat, one of the
girls injured when
Malala was, is
quick to laugh,
looks forward to
returning to school.
"I want to study. I
am not afraid." The
authorities are not
taking chances.
Armed policemen
have been deployed
in both Shazia's
and Kainat's home
and will escort
them to school.
Kainat's home is
hidden behind high
wall gates tucked
away in a neighbor-
hood of brown
cement buildings.
Armed police patrol,
eye everyone
suspiciously. Out
side Shazia's home
a policeman
wearing

a bullet proof
vest sits on a
plastic garden chair
with a kalashnikov
resting across
his knees, patroling
a nearby narrow
street that is flanked
by roaring fires
where vats of oil
and sticky sweets
are sold.

MANAWAR, MOTHER OF KAINAT

who was injured along with
Malala praised her
daughter's bravery and with
a smile says "she gets her
courage from me." Although
conservative and refusing
to have her picture taken,
Kainat's mother slammed
attacks on girl's education
and warned that Pakistan will
fail if girls are not educated.

NOW SHAZIA AND HER FRIEND KAIMAT ARE MAKING THEIR WAY BACK TO SCHOOL THROUGH HOLLY HOCKS AND LILACS

Riaz was also shot by
the Taliban gunman
who opened fire on
Malala near the Khusal
School for Girls. Shazia
and Kaimat were
wounded in a frenzy
of bullets too
but are back in school.
While Malala is not
there, to her friends in
her home town of
Mingora in the idyllic Swat
Valley she is a hero. 16
year old Kainat,
wrapped in a large
purple shawl and
sitting on a traditional rope bed
says Malala was very
brave and she was
friendly with everyone.

MALALA'S FRIENDS ARE BACK IN SCHOOL IN PAKISTAN

but for a month the
dreams keep
coming.
The voices, the
shots, the blood,
One young girl
shot by the same
Taliban bullets
returned last week
after a month in the
hospital. She has to
relearn how to use
her left
arm and hand. For
a long time she says
fear was in my
heart,
I couldn't stop it.
"But now I am not
afraid," she says,
self consciously,
rubbing her left
hand where a
bullet pierced
straight through
just below her thumb.

DESPITE A TRIBAL LAW FORBIDDING
THE KILLING OF WOMEN

and condemnation
for attacking
Malala, a defiant
Taliban called her a
spy of the West and
added, "we targeted
her because she
would speak against
the Taliban while
sitting with
shameless
strangers and idealized
the biggest enemy of
Islam, Barack
Obama."

FROM THE PROVINCE OF PUKTHUNKHWA

in Pakistan and now a
Senator in Canada,
Salma Ataullahjan,
from the same clan as
Malala, both
Yousafzai, share their
love of bright blues
and rose, colors in the
paintings the Senator
painted and has
hanging in her office. The
Senator's daughter was so
touched by Malala, she
wrote about their shared
heritage in a poem, how
they were brought up to
be warriors to fight for
honor. I think of her
imagining Malala, how
her namesake
fought the battle of
Maiwand, and how as a
child she did what most
grown men would not.
And remembered how
she blogged "I fear
nothing."

WHEN MALALA'S FATHER MET THE CANADIAN SENATOR

he was taken aback,
not only that she was
from Pakistan and
from the same
village but that she
spoke their native
language.
The Senator said
when my wife came
in and we sat down
and I turned to her
and spoke to her in
our mother tongue,
Pashto, she was
so surprised. She said
oh it's so nice to
have someone to speak
to me in Pashto.
The Canadian Senator
had been talking
at a conference in
Geneva and made the
personal decision
to take a detour to
Birmingham. She
has two adult
daughters
in Canada who are taken
with Malala's story.

One wrote a poem in
tribute that was read
on the Senate floor.
There is a photograph
of the Senator Salma
Ataullahjan with
Malala's father. There
is no name, no face
of Malala's mother.

SOMETIMES MAYBE IN ENGLAND

near 4 pm, getting
dark so early. The
lights going on, small
stars, dusky, dreaming.
I think of her in the
grey. Maybe she
wonders if she'd only
stayed,
held on to wanting to be
a doctor. She never
liked politics. What
if her father was wrong. What
if she should not
have listened to him.
She had always wanted
to take care of people. She
loved taking care of her
chickens and who
knows if they are still
living
or dead.

MALALA AWARDED WITH BRACER AWARD BY
WORLD PEACE AND PROSPERITY FOUNDATION

In her hospital bed
she hears the news,
that she won an award
from World Peace
and Prosperity for her
bravery and
commitment to
education for girls
in terrible conditions
in Swat Pakistan.
All the cards, the
gifts from strangers.
Soft cotton and
sweets.
Handmade lace and
drawings. Girls
younger than Malala
tell her their dreams,
how they love Pakistan but
want to leave it. They
send her dried petals
pressed in a book and
some afternoons
she would gladly give
back all this for
summers quiet and
slow, dozing
in the sun, leaves of

jasmine and
mulberry, dark jade
galanthus tree of
heaven,
before helicopters,
hiss of bullets, blast
of a gun.

FATWA ISSUED ON MALALA

not for her death
Choudary says but
because she is
used as a
propaganda tool
by US and
Pakistan. Fatwa.
Ugly word not
lyrical, not
musical
like "Malala" maybe
watching the last
leaves flutter
toward the river.
A grey sky day, a
glorious English
morning. "It is no
surprise what
happened to her
in Pakistan," the Taliban
hiss, "Malala is
mature Islamically."
They say if she allies
herself with America
and says her favorite
person is Barak
Obama and that she
does not want the
Sharia or the hjab,

wants to live under
a secular state,
she has put herself in
a very precarious
situation. All this for
the crime of
promoting education
for girls.

A BEAUTY STILL WAITING TO HEAL

but when I see her
eyes dancing in the
video I'm seeing
another person
for now. Eyes
flashing
electricity.
Nothing on her
isn't alive and fiery.
She's a warm fire,
smiling, she is
reading Rabindranath
Tagore, laughs
as she talks about
terror and
sadness. So many
girls afraid to
come to school.
So many nights
with no one
sleeping, coiled
into herself in
a white room
with a ruby
hanging.

62 PERCENT OF GIRLS IN PAKISTAN[2]

have never seen
the inside of a
school. Whether
or not Malala has
ever read
Aristotle, she
could only echo
his warning, "all
those who have
meditated on the
art of governing
mankind have
been convinced
that the fate of
empires depends
on the education
of its youth."

2 *Times of India Pakistan - Pakistan has failed in protecting the right of education for girls: Unesco by Manash Pratim Gohain, TNN Oct 20, 2012.*

OF COURSE SHE'D WANT

to know more about
the Birmingham
schools, how students
have so many choices.
One school started
in 1552. Time for
her country to
catch up she'd
frown.
She can't wait to
see Edgbaston High
School for girls and
Birmingham
Central Library, the
largest non-national
library in Europe.
And more than so
much else,
it can't hurt to
know she is at one
of the best
hospitals and she
is safe.

WHEN MALALA HEARS BIRMINGHAM IS HOME TO MANY RELIGIOUS, NATIONAL AND SPIRITUAL BELIEFS

She must feel sun
flood the pewter English
air: this is just what she
has been striving for.
She can't wait to be
well enough, strong
enough to move thru
the festival streets,
the Bangla Mela
and Vaisak Mela.
Sounds exotic.
There's so much
to know. If she
can heal as
miraculously fast
as she has survived,
I'm sure she would
love the International
Dance Festival and
Frankfort Christmas
market. All the lights

under the stars,
rhinestones and
diamond glitter,
and not having
to be watching in

the crowd for
someone
following her, even if

she wore flowers,
the wildest orange
rose and
sapphire, and
was singing.

MALALA'S DREAM OF ANIMALS

she falls asleep,
clutching a teddy
bear that morphs
into a lynx, a
leopard.
Some dreams aren't
nightmares but of
lush jade
mountains, conifers.
She dreams it is a place
of peace. She can lie
in the sun and
listen to the
Yellow Throated
Marten, Snow Cock and
Himalayan bear. In
her dream, she
lives in widening circles
where it's safe to
just watch pheasants
and falcons. In another
dream the musk
of mountain roses blooms
among wild
animals that would
never dream of
doing the horrible
things some men
do.

HINDU KUSH, THE RIVERS MEANDER THROUGH THIS VALLEY NOURISHIHG APPLES AND PERSIMMONS

when we see Malala with a
book, wrapped in bright cloth,
we hope she is reading and loving
the brightness she finds in
words and books. Hours to
daydream, to imagine Hindu
Kush, snow on the pines. The
apples and persimmon groves.
She doesn't want to remember
men and boys face down
on platforms, their legs held
so they wouldn't flop
around flogged,
convulsing under the
crack, the thud
of each lash,
hardly able to
stand up, shaking,
drenched in
tears.

THINKING OF THE DARK AMBER OF HER EYES

when the dark leaves twitch
and shimmer. When I think
of Malala, I think of a dark
eyed girl I taught years ago.
A high school class for, as
they called them, terminal
students. I was just out of
college with a degree in
English, no clues about
teaching it. The advanced
students were thrilling. It
didn't help I'd married a
month before and we
moved into an apartment
with a card table, a bed
and a cat I'd often
felt I'd gotten married to,
given a home to. No matter
the cat would run off the next
apartment we moved to
when I left this job
abruptly when someone
said "that looks like a
going away outfit" and it
was and I thought yes I am
going away today. What
reminds me so of Malala
was one of the many days I

had no control of this class,
the chaos and noise and
then in the back
of the room, her large eyes
pleading, Ramona, her
large eyes pleading,
raised her hands and said
"please everyone, I just want to learn."
Her IQ 70, her paper describing
the sounds and smells of a
burning barn the best in the
class, only one I remember.

AS IF THE DAYS HEALING

Watching the moon
wane about
Birmingham, the sky
turns clean and cold.
The stillness. This break
from death threats
published in
newspapers, slipped
under the door. This
pause, like trillium
plants under scorched
earth, nurtured in darkness,
waiting for new life, for
healing. Then the news,
summer of 2012, that
threat, still, to kill her.
Like those leaves burned
to ash,
she vows even if they come
to kill her, she will come
back, stronger than
ever and tell them
what they were trying
to do is brutal, wrong, that
education is a basic right,
unstoppable as new
flowers.

AS ROOTS OF NEW FLOWERS CAN'T HELP
BUT PUSH UP PAST DEAD LEAVES,
MALALA IS BLOOMING AGAIN:
(RECOVERY AND NEW BEGINNINGS)

IN MALALA'S SPRING DREAM

the pond is a dark blossom
unfolding. If she were to
move to the window in the
dream, there would be white
lilies thru blinds, suspended
instead of a moon.
Fog lips on roots
and willows filtering into
dreams of swans. The light
polishing water, connecting
what was behind her to
what's ahead.

MALALA UNDER THE SPREADING MULBERRY BRANCHES

sometimes she must want to
blend in with the dripping
roses and lilies, be ordinary
as a stone. Maybe even
dream of boys again. In this
space before whatever is
about to happen begins to, she
might want life to slow
down, be still as figures in a
tapestry, suspended in
warmth and beauty of the
garden, still as statues the
sun moves over and covers
then moves away and know
that like the light "success is
never final, failure is never
fatal, it's courage that counts."

IF AFTER SUCH A YEAR, MALALA CAN STILL SMILE

thrilled about being back in
school in Birmingham, excited to
have new friends, new
challenges,
who couldn't believe her dreams
will come true? She just
wants to be a normal teenage
girl and have the support of
other girls
around her. She wants to feel the
sun, smell the opening lilies
and roses, wants every girl to
feel not even bullets,
intimidation or death can stand
in the way of every girl to an
education. And
she wants them to feel, as she does
"When you arise in the morning,
think of what a precious privilege
it is to be alive — to breathe, to
think, to enjoy, to love."

AFTER SO MUCH TERROR, BEAUTY COMES INTO MALALA'S AFTERNOONS

After the morning rain, after
seas of umbrellas, the gardens
burst into poppies near the
River Rea. I can imagine
Malala curious, entranced by
daffodils and lambs Iris and
newborn horses, gardens of
rebirth, nests of new life and
the apple leaves bursting, so
many pale white flowers, violets,
birds she has no idea the
names for but is sure by the
time the sun sets she will.

WHEN MALALA WALKS NEAR THE RIVER

she smells willow roots,
grass clumped with feathers
that reminds her of the pet
chickens she left. No
birds no geese until
she looks deeper in the
reeds, sees goslings,
floating like pale cotton
batten or spun sugar.

NOT AS SUN DRENCHED AS THE HOME SHE LEFT

but light is coming
into swelling branches
in Binningham.
Malala misses her friends
but is bubbling with
joy to make new ones.
Sun on her skin, on her
lilac and rose cotton.
She wants to love
all things she is
about to discover:
smiling, sure "the
only thing that
makes a dream
impossible to
achieve is the fear of
failure."

AS THE ROOTS OF NEW FLOWERS

can't help but push their
brilliance up thru and past dead
leaves, Malala is blooming again.
That same impish smile, the light
in her more sparkling as the days
get longer again and she leaves
Queen Elizabeth Hospital in
February as the first Hepatica
leaves press up thru snow.
Her voice is stronger than
ever as she leaves for her
first time at Edgbaston High
School for Girls in Birmingham
on March 19. "I have achieved
my dream," the 15 year old smiled,
her pink knapsack over her shoulder,
her books her jewels. One of seven
featured on the cover of Time's
100 most influential people edition of
the magazine in April, she appeals to
people to vote for change. "One
vote can change Pakistan's
future. Gul Makai, that Pasto word for
corn flower, that name Malala took
from a folk tale has become
reality. She agreed to be that voice
against the Taliban and she will
never stop fighting for the rights
that must be free as air. "If we
want education, electricity and

natural gas in our country, we
must take a step," she said urging
people to vote in the election.
"Let's vote for our country.
We never realized how powerful
our vote is. It's our right,"
Malala appealed to the people.
"One day a change will come.
All boys and girls will be going
to schools and there will be
peace everywhere." I don't mind if
"I have to sit on the floor at
school. All I want
is education. I am not afraid."

BEFORE THE DAYS START TURNING LIGHT AGAIN

she drifts thru mists
that will bring new
mornings like bright
ness from old pain
boxes, still wild to
learn more of the
world. She wants to
take back her name
from colleges who
honor her for now.
She needs a little more
time, insists to be
photographed only
with a book in her
hands so people will
know she loves what
some have not loved
enough, valued
enough; wrapping
flame rose scarves
around her to
cover the damage.

WHEN MORE AND MORE CHILDREN
HEAR ABOUT MALALA

most are shocked,
many think they
would never take
risks like that.
Some say in their
country people
moan about going
to school but she
risked so much.
Brave, fearless, "I
hadn't thought
things like this
possible
in our time." Some
wonder how their
country will be
perceived.
"Deeply moved,"
"I would
like to know her." One
said "Lebanon is
an unstable
country. People are
helpless and
insecure and this
image is seen all

over the Arab
world." Another
says "What are our
rights? Nobody
knows." But because
of Malala, they are
inspired.

Lyn Lifshin's *Another Woman Who Looks Like Me* was published by Godine/Black SparrowBooks, October, 2006. Also out in 2006, her prize winning book about the famous, short lived, beautiful race horse, Ruffian; *The Licorice Daughter: My Year With Ruffian* from Texas Review Press. Lifshin's other books include *Before it's Light* by Black Sparrow Press, following their publication of *Cold Comfort; 92 Rapple Drive* Coatlism Press; *Lost in the Fog* by Finishing Line Press; *Light at the End: The Jesus Poems; Katrina* published by Poetic Matrix Press; *Ballet Madonnas; Tsunami as History; Lost Horses; Drifting;* and *In Mirrors.* For other books, bio, photographs see her website: www.lynlifshin.com. *Persephone* was published by Red Hen Press; Texas Review published *Barbaro, Beyond Brokenness.* Most recent books: *Ballroom; All the Poets (Mostly) Who Have Touched me, Living and Dead, All True, Especially the Lies; Knife Edge* & *Absinthe: The Tango Poems.* October 1, 2013, NYQ Books published *A Girl Goes into The Woods.* Also, *For the Roses: Poems Inspired by Joni Mitchell.* Recently published *Hitchcock Hotel.* Forthcoming: *Secretariat: The Red Freak, the Miracle; Malala; The Tangled Alphabet: Istanbul Poems* and *Luminous Women: Eneduanna, Scheherazade and Nefertiti;* an ebook of *Marilyn Monroe* from Rubber Boots Press, and a dvd of the film *Lyn Lifshin: Not Made of Glass.*

PRESS PRODUCERS

SUPPORTER OF THE PRESS
- Deepest gratitude

Susan Reichardt
Lavonne Westbrooks
PJ Sheridan
Primo Poets
Judith Tucker
Linda Milks
Katelin Holloway
SE Bradley
Laura Townsend
Rebecca Hubbard
Magick

Shawna Swetech
Lillian Schuller
Michael Milosch
Zachary Ritter
Chris Biszewski
James friend
Miles Peterson
Susan Dullack
Mary Motary
Anonymous

SPONSOR OF THE PRESS
- Profound Appreciation

J. Glenn & Barbara Evans
Joyce Downs
Nicole Woo
Barb Jiminez
Sylvia Levinson
Tricia Ferguson
Edward Maupin
Diane

Grace Grafton
Richard Kovac
Charles Elston
Jon Allen
Sharon Bard
Kelly Gazaway
Anonymous

PATRON OF THE PRESS
- Keen Affection

Sandy Stillwell
Chris Hoffman
Paul Dolinsky
Tomas Gayton
The Entrekin Foundation
Joseph Milosch
Carina Wagner

Joseph Campbell
julie1
Peggy Gregory
Anne Whitehouse
Albert G. Jordan
Anonymous

PRESS PRODUCERS

I would like to thank all of those who worked on and participated in our *Summer 2013 Season of Poetry* campaign to raise finances for this and two other volumes of poetry. Thanks to Devon Peterson, James Downs, Joyce Downs, and Dan Davis. Also, the three poets Lyn Lifshin, Raphael Block and Joseph Milosch. And of course all of these people who contributed so ready to this effort. Small poetry press publishing is a joy to do but certainly cost money and these Producers, like in any artistic effort, are the ones who make it posswible. Thank you!
— John Peterson, Publisher

www.ingramcontent.com/pod-product-compliance
Lightning Source LLC
Chambersburg PA
CBHW030839090426
42737CB00009B/1039